OVER the Moon

COMPLETE PRIMARY ENGLISH LANGUAGE PRO...

GW01395845

Home

Mary O'Keeffe

g GILL EDUCATION

Wakey wakey! Ella has to get up and get ready for her first day of school! Can you help Ella to find 5 things that she needs to get ready this morning?

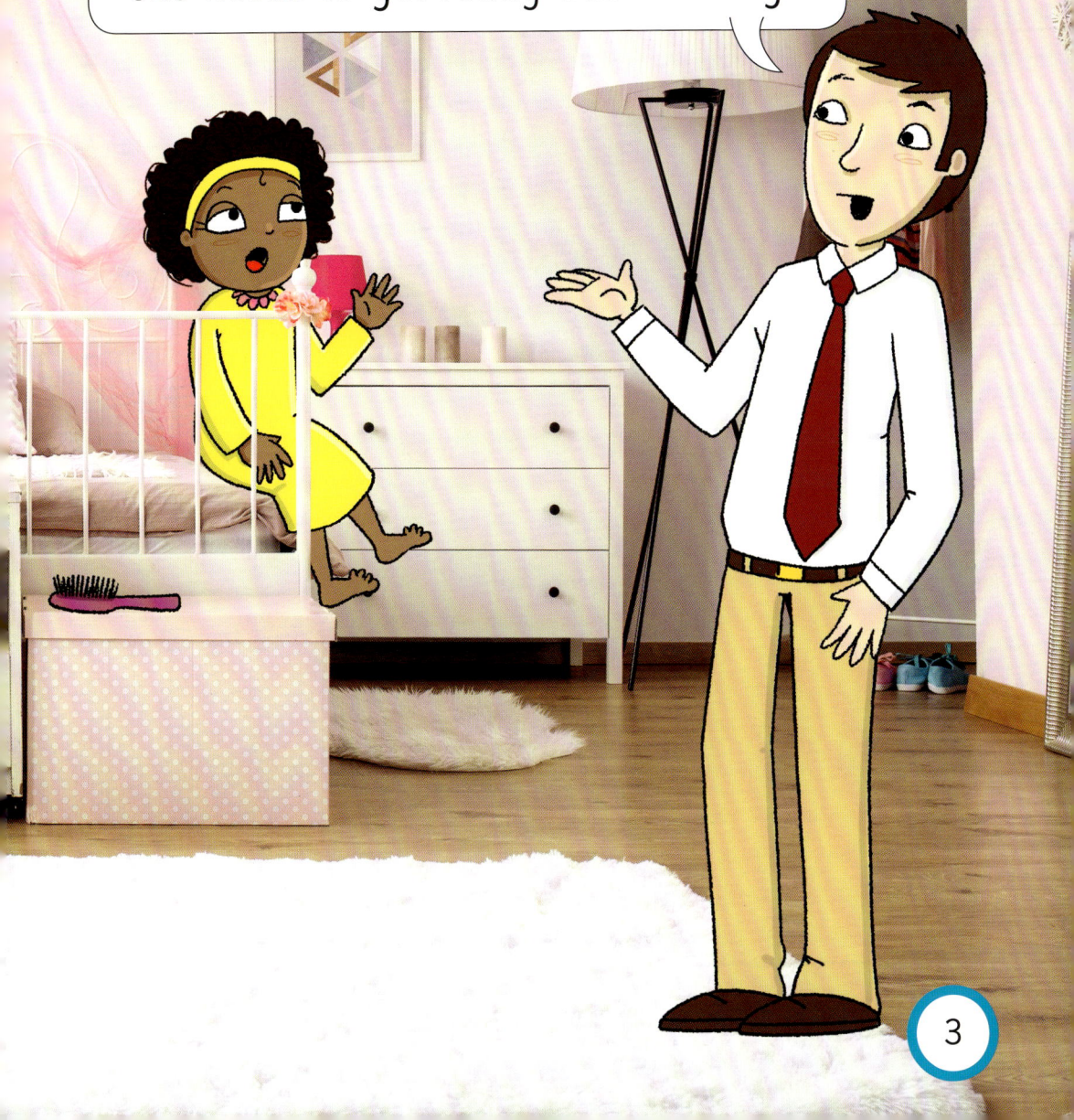

We just love breakfast! Mam and Dad always say breakfast is the most important meal of the day! What will we eat for breakfast?

There are lots of utensils in the kitchen drawer! Ella wants to eat a yoghurt before school.

- Which can she use to eat the yoghurt?
- Which utensil might you use to slice a pizza?
- Can you find a rolling pin for pastry?
- Can you find the whisk for whipping cream?
- Which utensil might you use to stir porridge?

While Evan and Ella are eating their breakfast, Dad or I will make their lunch. Look at Evan's lunch box. What will he have today? What might Ella have for her lunch?

Can you help Ella get ready? What does she need to do before going to school?

Evan and Ella are going to be late if they don't hurry up!

Can you help Evan and Ella to make sure they are ready for school?

Right, let's go to school!

Which kind of transport might Ella and Evan use to get to school?

We're walking to school today! The weather is so nice in September! What's the safest way for Evan and Ella to cross the road?